CM0092162B

LOVE LOVE

Don't just pretend to love others...
really love them.

Derek and Kylie Gerrard

Love Love.
Don't just pretend to love people... really love them.

Published by BTC Publishing
a division of Be The Church Ltd
PO Box 403 Scarborough WA 6922
Australia

ISBN 978-0-9874141-0-6 (print)
ISBN 978-0-9874141-1-3 (eBook)

www.lovelove.org.au
www.bethechurch.org.au

This book is dedicated to all those people who are living out what it means to Be The Church.

Contents

PART A
Love Love

Chapter One

Why love love?

When Jesus was asked what the greatest of all His commandments were, He answered by saying love God and love other people. Later Paul said don't just pretend to love people... really love them. This is the foundation of Love Love.

A few years ago we started the journey of trying to stop pretending to love people and really love them. To remove things in our life that made us focus on ourselves. To be honest about our prejudices and put ourselves in situations that caused us to challenge and overcome these mindsets. To try different ways of practically loving other people, while learning how to respond to those who were deeply impacted by our love and also those who wanted to take advantage of our generosity. To see whether really loving people could point them towards God, in a way that they would want their own relationship with Him.

That journey has seen us plant a church in Scarborough, Western Australia, where a community has gathered to love God together and out of that, motivate one another to live a lifestyle of loving other people in practical ways. (You can check that out at www.bethechurch.org.au). We have also been on countless mission trips to India, Vanuatu, the Philippines and to Aboriginal communities within Australia, all with a desire to love the poor, the needy, the marginalised and those suffering injustice.

The whole premise is built on the idea that by loving people in practical ways, we can demonstrate the love of God to them.

This book actually started as a list of practical ideas that people in our church could use. After our Sunday service, our church engages in different activities that allow us to impact our community in a positive way. Our small groups also run projects in their neighbourhoods throughout the year and we are regularly looking for ideas that each person can do in the marketplace - the place where God has them in the community - like school, university, business or government.

The list grew to about 200 ideas, so we thought we needed to categorise them to make it easier for people to find what they were looking for. We then thought other Christian groups and churches might be able to use that list if we were able to put it together as a resource. Add a bit of context and some stories of our journey and here we are.

Before we begin, we want to thank all of the amazing people God has brought into our church community to do this journey with us. We've done some crazy things and they are always putting themselves out there, serving other people for nothing in return. We have seen people get saved through this work, some come off drugs, alcohol and other addictions, smiles on people's faces as they have a good meal or conversation and tears because of someone's generosity.   On the whole, the reward for these people is knowing that they are fulfilling what God has called all Christians to do - simply love other people.

A final word before we begin. If you have the eBook version of this book you should have received it for free, or if you have the printed version you should not have paid more than cost price. This is our gift to you, to encourage you to find innovative ways to love other people, as a way of demonstrating God's love to them. If you see value in this book and would have been happy to pay for it, then we'd love you to use that money towards your first Love Love idea - by demonstrating love to someone in your world in a practical way. We'd also like you to share any ideas you have on our website at www.lovelove.org.au so that we can continue to learn from one another.

Chapter Two

It really works

Recently we had a phone call from a young man that we'll call Peter. Peter had moved to Australia to try and have a fresh start in life. Unfortunately, he became involved with the wrong crowd and ended up living on the street, with no work and spending most of his time drinking.

We ran an event after church each week called "Life on the Green", where we would give away hamburgers, as well as provide clothes and books to those who needed them. It is one of the ways we could get our whole church serving the community in a practical way. We also had a group that had started playing a weekly game of touch rugby, as a way of connecting to many of the young street people in the area. Peter regularly came down for a hamburger, had taken many of the clothes and books and usually came down to play touch rugby. Over time Peter even started venturing into our church services, so we got to know him pretty well.

He would regularly ask why we did all this "stuff" for free. Consistently people in the church would tell him that God loved him and we were just finding practical ways to show him that.

The last conversation we had with Peter was trying to convince him to go down to the police station, to admit to a crime he had just committed, as we had heard the police were looking for him. We had offered to go with him, but then hadn't heard from him for about three months, until we got this phone call.

Peter was very excited when he phoned us to say that since we last spoke, his life had been transformed and it was all because of God. The police had caught up with him, but he had subsequently got himself a job, had got off the street and into his own home and had stopped drinking. He started telling us how he now knew that God loved him and had provided for him and that he wanted to start helping other people. A week later Peter came around to our house where we had one of our small groups meeting and it was literally like talking to a different person. God was all over him.

It's one of many stories we've seen, where simply loving someone in a practical way demonstrated God's love to them, to the point that they started their own relationship with Him and their life was transformed.

Chapter Three

What started in Vanuatu...

Many years ago we were asked to lead a short-term mission trip to Vanuatu. It was the first time we had done anything like this. While Vanuatu sounds like a tropical holiday destination, it's also a place with a lot of poverty. It only seemed natural that while we were there we would try and do something practical to help those who were less fortunate than us. An opportunity presented for us to help fund and build a water tank for the small island community we were visiting. If water supply on this island ran out, they would have to take a boat ride to the mainland to get fresh water, which in very dry seasons could be a matter of life or death.

Building the water tank required both our team and locals on the island to work together. As we did this there were many opportunities for conversations which inevitably led to people asking "Why are you doing this?" or "Did you pay for yourself to come here?" As the days went by, the conversation would get onto deeper topics like "Who is this God you keep talking about?"

We didn't see anyone come to know Jesus on this trip, but it made us realise that a simple act of loving someone in a practical way, gave a foundation to build a trusting relationship and out of that place, came meaningful conversations about life.

Once we returned home, that trip shifted a number of things in us that caused us to rethink how we were living.

Firstly, we were confronted with the reality of poverty. We were reasonably well off at the time and while we thought we were generous, we had also just had a holiday to an island on the Whitsundays that was so exclusive you needed to hire a helicopter to fly there. Suffice to say we were still indulging in our own pleasures and there was room to get a different balance.   This instantly changed after our first hand experience of third-world living conditions and we realised that no matter how we looked at it, on a global scale we were wealthy. We knew that we needed to reorient our lives to use our money generously, in helping the poor and marginalised and to see God's kingdom grow.

We were also confronted with the reality of many people just "going" to church rather than "being" the church. In other words, we knew people who attended a church service on Sunday, spent time with their Christian friends and then went and lived a similar life to everyone else in society from Monday to Saturday. There was an apathy and complacency of people in churches towards having an active faith that was burdened for the lost, in a way that motivated them to reach out and engage with people on a day-to-day basis.   They had lost sight of the scriptures where God calls us to look after "the least of these", where we practically help the poor, the needy and the marginalised.

We realised that part of this was because as a society, we are constantly surrounded by media and marketing that says we are the most important people in the world. Materialism, consumerism, individualism, rationalism, hedonism and any other "ism" that makes the focus about us and not about Christ or other people, is what we are dealing with every day. Very direct and overt advertising that says you deserve this, or it's time to get the faster, smaller, shinier model because the old one won't do. We normalise our behaviour towards these messages, because we live like everyone around us, rather than fighting for this radical life of following Jesus, where our life is actually lived to the fullest when we surrender it to him.

Jesus said that:

"If any of you wants to be my follower, you must turn from your selfish ways, take up your cross daily, and follow me. If you try to hang on to your life, you will lose it. But if you

give up your life for my sake, you will save it. And what do you benefit if you gain the whole world but are yourself lost or destroyed? If anyone is ashamed of me and my message, the Son of Man will be ashamed of that person when he returns in his glory and in the glory of the Father and the holy angels." (Luke 9:23-27)

What we were encountering was a combination of churches and society that were creating passive audiences, rather than empowered ministers, who could "be the church" outside the four walls of a church building.

We are still searching for the answers to many of these questions, but that one trip to Vanuatu has set us on a course where God has called us to not just pretend to love other people, but really love them.

A good way to sum this up is by what James wrote in regards to faith in action:

"What good is it, dear brothers and sisters, if you say you have faith but don't show it by your actions? Can that kind of faith save anyone? Suppose you see a brother or sister who has no food or clothing, and you say, 'Good-bye and have a good day, stay warm and eat well' - but then you don't give that person any food or clothing. What good does that do? So you see, faith by itself isn't enough. Unless it produces good deeds, it is dead and useless. Now someone may argue,

'Some people have faith, others have good deeds.' But I say, 'How can you show me your faith if you don't have good deeds? I will show you my faith by my good deeds.'"

(James 2:14-18)

Chapter Four

God first loved you

Before we get into all the practical things we can do to love people, we need to set the right foundation - that God first loved us.

"We love each other because God first loved us."

(1 John 4:19)

The core of the entire Gospel message is that God loves you and me. The love that we show to other people can only be because God first loved us. In fact, let's be honest, if that wasn't the case, why would we naturally choose to love other people like this anyway?

John had earlier described what love looked like. He said:

"We know what real love is because Jesus gave up his life for us. So we also ought to give up our lives for our brothers and sisters. If someone has enough money to live well and sees a brother or sister in need but shows no compassion - how can God's love be in that person? Dear children, let's not merely say that we love each other, let us show the truth by our actions." (1 John 3: 16-18)

Part of our response to God's love for us has to be about loving other people and as John says, this is a tangible love in action.

A lot of the things we do to love people involve us giving something away or volunteering our time for free. It's about sacrifice - giving up part of our life for someone else. Often we are asked why we would do that, as these people may have never been loved that way before, may have never noticeably felt the love of God or may have a pre-conceived idea of what a Christian is like.

We believe the scriptures are clear that we need to do practical things for people in need. Our response to their questions are always that God loves them and this is our way of showing it.

Chapter Five
Now love one another

With the foundation that God first loved us, there is another point we need to make before we talk directly about loving others.

Jesus said:

> *"So I am now giving you a new commandment: Love each other. Just as I have loved you, you should love each other. Your love for one another will prove to the world that you are my disciples." (John 13: 34-35)*

In other words people will know that we are followers of Jesus by our love for other followers of Jesus. We need to love one another.

Paul wrote to the Galatians:

> *"Therefore, whenever we have the opportunity, we should do good to everyone - especially to those in the family of faith." (Galatians 6:10)*

This has some practical applications. The first is that if we are unable to love other followers of Jesus, then it doesn't set a great example when we start reaching out to love other people.

The second is that we are meant to look after other believers so that collectively our needs are being met, we are being cared for and supported on an emotional, physical and spiritual level. If a fellow believer is trying to reach out to love others, but is not in a healthy state themselves because of unmet personal needs, there is the possibility that in helping others they may become resentful and actually negatively impact their own well being.

The early followers of Jesus lived out the reality of looking after each other in very practical ways. We read in Acts that:

> *"All the believers met together in one place and shared everything they had.   They sold their property and possessions and shared the money with those in need."*
>
> *(Acts 2: 44-45)*

Paul also talked about this idea when speaking of generosity to the Corinthian church. He said:

> *"Yes, you will be enriched in every way so that you can always be generous.   And when we take your gifts to those who need them, they will thank God.   So two good things will result from this ministry of giving - the needs of the believers in Jerusalem will be met, and they will joyfully express their thanks to God." (2 Corinthians 9: 11-12)*

One of our closest friends over the last 20 years is a guy we will call John.   At different times throughout our friendship we had talked about God, but that had never resulted in John wanting to come to church or become a Christian.

He often talked about coming along on one of our mission trips and while it had little spiritual context he liked the idea of going to a poor community, getting a different perspective on life and doing what he could, to help people less fortunate than himself.

On one of our trips to India, John decided he would come. We were excited that he was coming but also quite apprehensive as it was the first time we had taken a not-yet-Christian as part of the team. We became nervous about what he might think during the times we sang or prayed together, or when we prayed for other people.   In preparation we bought him a Bible and suggested he read Mark and Acts saying "that's the kind of stuff we will be doing."

While we were on the trip John gave his heart to the Lord. It was amazing to see one of our best friends choose to follow Jesus and it was a very humbling experience to have a small part to play in his journey.

A little side note here - if you have been praying for the salvation of friends or family for many years - don't give up. We have to continue to believe and not get complacent about seeing those closest to us coming to know God. We should never get tired of reaching out to them, as even after many years we may still be the best people to help them find God.   While it may feel like it is never going to happen, we need to keep the reality of their eternal destination at the forefront of our minds.

Not long after this happened, we asked John what it was that made him believe in Jesus, given that it hadn't happened in all the years before when we had talked about God. His answer struck us and is really the point of this story. He said that it made no sense for a group of random people, from all generations, with nothing in common other than their love for God, to spend their own money and give up their time to come and help other people.   What stood out for him was that when we were together at team times, the love that people had for each other was so overwhelming. It was that love for one another that helped him experience the reality of God in a tangible way.

What amazed us was that he had come on this trip to find a way to love other people and the result was that by being around Christians and seeing their love for one another, he found God. It is so important that as we reach out to love others, we are first loving one another.

Chapter Six
Why love other people?

We believe that as you learn to love God more, you can't help but have a heart to love other people. Throughout the scriptures we refer to in this book, it is clear that when God's people love other people, this demonstrates the heartbeat of God in a very real and tangible way.

Many times in scripture this love is described as a practical love. Isaiah says this well:

> "No, this is the kind of fasting I want. Free those who are wrongly imprisoned, lighten the burden of those who work for you. Let the oppressed go free, and remove the chains that bind people. Share your food with the hungry, and give shelter to the homeless. Give clothes to those who need them, and do not hide from relatives who need your help."
>
> (Isaiah 58: 6-7)

Paul talks a lot about loving others and says that anything else we do in our spiritual journey means nothing unless it is founded in loving others:

> "If I could speak all the languages of earth and of angels, but didn't love others, I would only be a noisy gong or a clanging cymbal. If I had the gift of prophecy, and if I understood all of God's secret plans and possessed all knowledge, and if I

had such faith that I could move mountains, but didn't love others, I would be nothing. If I gave everything I have to the poor and even sacrificed my body, I could boast about it, but if I didn't love others, I would have gained nothing."

(1 Corinthians 13: 1-3)

Jesus himself talked about loving people in practical ways:

"Then they will reply, 'Lord, when did we ever see you hungry or thirsty or a stranger or naked or sick or in prison, and not help you?' And he will answer, 'I tell you the truth, when you refused to help the least of these my brothers and sisters, you were refusing to help me.'" (Matthew 25:44-45)

What we find interesting is that within most people, whether they are Christian or not, there is an innate desire to help other people. So often when we are running practical love ideas as a church, members of the community will come and ask how they can get involved or if they can donate different things to our activities.

This idea of loving people is not just about generic acts of kindness. If we really love people, then ultimately we want to see them in a relationship with Christ, knowing that at that point they will be able to live their life to the fullest, as their eternal future is secured. We have to make sure that this is not just about us looking for great things to do in our community, but that we are constantly pointing people towards Jesus, giving Him all the glory, all the praise and all the honour.

What we have learnt though, is that this practical love is an effective way of introducing people to God. Finding ways to practically love people nudges them towards God in a non-confronting way, that removes the preconceptions of religion or other methods of evangelism. We have found that people are often humbled when something is given to them, rather than them being asked to give something.

The act of love is not a pushy, "bible-bashing" evangelism style and yet often presents an opportunity for deeper conversation.

As sad as it is, some people have not had good interactions with other Christians and if nothing else, these acts of love, leave people with a more positive impression of Christianity than they may have had before.

Many of the ideas we have presented can be done in a group so they also present simple ways that Christians can encourage each other to get involved in evangelism.

As the writer of Hebrews says:

"Let us think of ways to motivate one another to acts of love and good works." (Hebrews 10:24)

When we looked into our community to find where some of the needs were, one of the more obvious places was a group of homeless people. While we first assumed that the way to help them was by providing a place to stay, or providing them with meals, this turned out to be an incorrect assumption. Their primary needs were actually a desire for conversation and having a place where they belong. When we were giving away hamburgers many of the homeless community would prefer to come and cook and serve the food, offering a service to the community themselves, rather than just eating the food.

There was one man in that group, who we will call James. A few times a week we would go and find James and just have a thirty minute conversation with him, as a very simple way of meeting one of his needs. It turned out that James was a very good guitarist, but his guitar had been broken. As a church we decided to buy James a guitar and it was an amazing experience giving this to him, as he cried and shared that no one had ever thought of him that way before. Unfortunately, a few days after we gave James the guitar, he ended up in prison. Initially we felt a bit despondent, but as the scriptures suggest, we decided to visit him in prison. When we arrived James cried again, overwhelmed that we would care enough to come and visit him. James articulated how he wanted to change his life and that he knew it was time to break the poverty cycle he had been in. We prayed together that he would be able to get out of prison and into a drug rehabilitation program, which is what eventuated.

Eleven months later James randomly arrived in church. He was just about to complete the drug rehabilitation course and believed his addiction had been broken, having not had alcohol or drugs during that time. He wanted to come and visit the church to say thanks for the love and care that we had shown him. He gave thanks to God, knowing that God loved him, because these strangers in his life had shown him love. His response was that he wanted to know God more and find practical ways he could start loving other people.

The ultimate heart behind loving other people is a heart of generosity. It's about putting others before yourself, being prepared to use your own time and resources for the benefit of other people.

Being generous with other people is one of the greatest examples we can give of demonstrating God's love to others.

Paul wrote about generosity:

"Remember this, a farmer who plants only a few seeds will

get a small crop. But the one who plants generously will get a generous crop. You must each decide in your heart how much to give. And don't give reluctantly or in response to pressure. For God loves a person who gives cheerfully. And God will generously provide all you need. Then you will always have everything you need and plenty left over to share with others." (2 Corinthians 9:6-8)

We've seen so much generosity from people in the short journey we've been on and it never ceases to amaze us. It doesn't even need to be something extravagant or expensive, as there is a real impact when you see someone genuinely give something of themselves. On one end of the spectrum we've seen one of the children in our church wrap up coins in encouraging notes to give to people on the street. At the other end, someone bought a car for the church, to make it available for people to borrow at no charge, where they had a need with short term transport. One cost fifty cents and the other cost thousands of dollars but all of these acts of love are generous and they all impact lives. It's the heart of generosity that counts.

We love other people because Jesus proclaimed it and He demonstrated it. As a Christian, if we are doing our best to live a life like Jesus, then we have to love other people. Jesus commissioned us saying that:

"I tell you the truth, anyone who believes in me will do the same works I have done, and even greater works, because I am going to be with the Father." (John 14:12)

You may be the only "Jesus" that people get to meet. Reaching out to others, loving people and pointing them towards God is not just for the people who work in a Christian organisation or who have a gift of evangelism - it's for every follower of Jesus. Paul said to Timothy that we should all do the work of an evangelist:

"But you should keep a clear mind in every situation. Don't be afraid of suffering for the Lord. Work at telling others the Good News, and fully carry out the ministry God has given you." (2 Timothy 4:5)

There are some people in this world that only you will be able to reach. You gifts, your passions, your generation, your place in the world, your experience and your relationships all come together for the sake of the salvation of other people. Paul describes this by saying that we reflect the glory of God:

"So all of us who have had that veil removed can see and reflect the glory of the Lord. And the Lord - who is the Spirit - makes us more and more like him as we are changed into his glorious image." (2 Corinthians 3:18)

He then goes on to say that we represent God and He is

making His appeal to people through us as His ambassadors:

> *"So we are Christ's ambassadors. God is making his appeal through us. We speak for Christ when we plead, 'Come back to God!'" (2 Corinthians 5:20)*

Chapter Seven

What happens when it doesn't work?

So far we have told the success stories. In reality, with many of the people we interact with, they either give little response or in some cases take advantage of the generosity that is being provided.

It's an important point that we don't want to ignore - what happens when practically loving people doesn't work?

One of the people we have worked with is a guy we will call Ben. Ben came into our church one week and started getting involved with some of the outreach work we were doing. Ben was unemployed and living on the street. Over a period of time the people in our community helped Ben get a job, someone lent him a car, some people helped him with accommodation and he was given countless meals. It could only be described as extravagant generosity that was poured upon him. During that time he gave his life to the Lord and he was baptised.

At one point, Ben went missing for about a week, with the car that he had been lent. We phoned the local hospitals, checked with some of his friends and eventually registered him as a missing person. We believed that with the life transformation he had been living, something tragic must have happened. We received a call after a week from an acquaintance of his who we had contacted, as they had heard that he had been seen at the casino the night before. As it happened, we were at a show at the casino the following night and although we were still in disbelief, thought we would take a walk and see if we could find Ben. We prayed that if God wanted us to still spend time loving Ben that we would find him. You can imagine our heartbreak (and the shock on his face) when we walked straight into the casino, down an aisle of poker machines and found him.

Up until that point it all sounds like a great story, but although we continued to try and help him, it turned out that Ben had a drug and gambling addiction that he wasn't prepared to give up. After the casino incident we didn't seen Ben for a while, until recently we heard from him and he said that he was still wanting to sort life out and get right with God. That's what we are believing for Ben and we will continue to do what we can to help him, for as long as the journey takes.

Many people would look at that situation and say that we are being taken for granted. That the time and resources we have put into one person's life is not worth it. It could easily result in us being more selective with who we work with, or the types of activities we do with certain people.

Obviously we need to apply wisdom and there are certainly boundaries with Ben that are a lot tighter than when we first met him, but the point is that we will still continue to love him in very practical ways.

During this time we really sought God about removing ourselves from Ben's life but God spoke clearly to us about the parable of the lost sheep:

> *"If a man has a hundred sheep and one of them wanders away, what will he do? Won't he leave the ninety-nine others on the hills and go out to search for the one that is lost? And if he finds it, I tell you the truth, he will rejoice over it more than over the ninety-nine that didn't wander away! In the same way, it is not my heavenly Father's will that even one of these little ones should perish." (Matthew 18: 12-14)*

What we realised is that Jesus never gives up on us. He does the journey with us for as long as it takes. We started to comprehend that Jesus is taken for granted by people, including us, on so many occasions and He was aware of that even when he completed the greatest act of love in the history of the world. He continues to extend that grace, mercy and love to us over and over again.

When you read how Jesus modelled treating people like

this, He continued to love them and encourages us to do the same thing:

> *"But to you who are willing to listen, I say, love your enemies! Do good to those who hate you. Bless those who curse you. Pray for those who hurt you. If someone slaps you on one cheek, offer the other cheek also. If someone demands your coat, offer your shirt also. Give to anyone who asks and when things are taken away from you, don't try to get them back. Do to others as you would like them to do to you. If you love only those who love you, why should you get credit for that? Even sinners love those who love them! And if you do good only to those who do good to you, why should you get credit? Even sinners do that much! And if you lend money only to those who can repay you, why should you get credit? Even sinners will lend to other sinners for a full return. Love your enemies! Do good to them. Lend to them without expecting to be repaid. Then your reward from heaven will be very great, and you will truly be acting as children of the Most High, for he is kind to those who are unthankful and wicked. You must be compassionate, just as your Father is compassionate." (Luke 6: 27-36)*

This is something that can be really hard to live out. What Jesus says goes totally against what people expect and how our society usually responds.

Paul shared some similar words with the Romans:

> *"Never pay back evil with more evil. Do things in such a way that everyone can see you are honourable. Do all that you can to live in peace with everyone. Dear friends, never take revenge. Leave that to the righteous anger of God. For the Scriptures say, 'I will take revenge; I will pay them back,' says the Lord. Instead, 'If your enemies are hungry, feed them. If they are thirsty, give them something to drink. In doing this, you will heap burning coals of shame on their heads.' Don't let evil conquer you, but conquer evil by doing good." (Romans 12:17-21)*

Our response is that we need to keep loving people, even when it hurts.   If people don't appreciate the love we are showing them, it doesn't matter, God appreciates it.

Chapter Eight

Local or international?

One of the good questions to ask when you start finding practical ways to love people is whether you should do it locally or overseas.

In one of our overseas trips we ended up in a small village community in the Philippines. We had almost finished our trip, when the people we were staying with told us about a group of people living on a local rubbish tip, that they would go down once a week and provide a meal for. They invited us to go with them and to this day, this is still one of the most confronting things we have done. There was about a hundred people that lived there and they had built their homes out of things from the rubbish tip. Most of the children were not dressed and when we arrived with the meal, they lined up with broken bowls and containers that they had also found on the rubbish tip. Of all the people we have encountered in our travels, these were the poorest of the poor.

We had offered to pay for the meal that night, as our way of contributing to their work and apologised because it was the end of our trip and we only had $80 left. The lady who ran the team we were staying with began to cry and thanked us because that $80 would feed the community of one hundred people for the next three months. It was even more sobering when we arrived home a few days later and did a small shop at our grocery store to top up the cupboard. We spent $150 on food for the two of us that wouldn't even last one week. That same amount of money would have fed the community that lived on the rubbish tip for six months.

We realise that income and living costs are very different in all parts of the world, but this trip gave us a new perspective on what it means for us to go into the nations. There is a level of poverty not experienced in our own nation and we have the opportunity to generously provide for the poor and demonstrate God's love to them. With that said, we believe that practically loving people needs to start at home.

Jesus gave a clear indication that we should focus locally and internationally:

> *"Jesus came and told his disciples, 'I have been given all authority in heaven and on earth. Therefore, go and make disciples of all the nations, baptizing them in the name of the Father and the Son and the Holy Spirit.'"*
>
> *(Matthew 28:18-19)*

Later, just before He ascended to heaven, Jesus said:

"But you will receive power when the Holy Spirit comes upon you. And you will be my witnesses, telling people about me everywhere - in Jerusalem, throughout Judea, in Samaria, and to the ends of the earth." (Acts 1:8)

Keep in mind these are some of the few instructions Jesus gave us after His resurrection, which says something of their importance.

It is clear that we are called to the nations and we have used these verses as a model for how we get there. Jerusalem was the hometown of the people that Jesus was speaking to, Judea and Samaria were their neighbouring areas and the ends of the earth refers to other nations.

We started our work in our own neighbourhood, our Jerusalem. We believe this is the place you spend most of your time, where you have the opportunity to build your strongest relationships. It's the place where you have neighbours, where you can interact with local businesses, local schools and local government agencies. Your neighbourhood is the place where you naturally engage with people in the everyday and can find simple and regular ways to love people.

Once we had people mobilised in our own neighbourhood, we began to pray for a surrounding area that God was calling us to, and from there, another nation.

This ended up being some indigenous communities in the northern parts of Australia and then India. In these locations we have found that partnering with local churches and Christian organisations helps provide a sustainable model of support. They maintain the day-to-day relationships with the people we are reaching out to. We can support them financially and by sending teams that encourage them, we help lift their profile and support them in the mission God has called them to.

Chapter Nine

Servant evangelism or power evangelism?

The last point we want to make is the difference between the concept of servant evangelism and power evangelism.

Servant evangelism is a common phrase used to describe the type of outreach we have talked about in the book so far. Steve Sjogren has written some excellent material on the topic. It is the idea that by serving other people, by finding acts of love, we can practically demonstrate the love of God to them. It may get them to think about God in a different way, it could challenge some of their existing mindsets, and in many cases it may be the foundation of a relationship that begins and continues as we point people towards God.

We have said that to ultimately love people is to see them in a relationship with God, knowing at the point they receive Christ as their Lord and Saviour they will live their life to the fullest. While one way of loving people is through a practical love, another way is by responding to the Holy Spirit, believing that in a moment, someone can have an encounter with the living God that will change their life.

This is the idea of power evangelism, a term first coined

by John Wimber.   He said that it is "evangelism that transcends the rational through the demonstration of God's power in signs and wonders and introduces the numinous of God."

Jesus made the blind see, the deaf hear, the lame walk, healed the sick, raised the dead, stilled the storm, multiplied fish and loaves and many more signs and wonders that are still happening today. We need to listen to the Holy Spirit's promptings. We need to have the faith that God will heal someone when we pray for them, that God can give us prophetic words for people, or words of wisdom and discernment, that we can cast out demons and live the supernatural life that Jesus died for and that we were intended for.

Both servant evangelism and power evangelism are about presenting the Gospel and equally play a part in pointing people towards God.

Chapter Ten
Love. It's simple really.

We hope that our few short stories have inspired you to find practical ways to love people in the context of where God has placed you in the world.

We hope that you can find like-minded people that will motivate one another to demonstrate the love of God to others.

We hope that as you do this you will find that your relationship with God continues to grow and that what is on God's heart for your community is what gets on your heart.

We hope that you won't just pretend to love people – but that you will really love them.

Start simple - just make sure that you start.

PART B
A Practical Guide

How to use the practical guide

We want to provide you with practical ideas on simple ways that you can love other people. This is just a starting list and will hopefully encourage you to come up with your own too.

We have provided some guidelines to help you succeed. Many of these come from things we got wrong, so please learn from our mistakes!

We have put the ideas into categories that are scripturally based on the different areas God calls us to love other people.

There are over 200 ideas and in case that is too overwhelming, we have also added two top 5 lists. These are what we think are the simplest and most effective ideas, with one list being things you can do on your own and the other list being things you can do with other people.

Some guidelines

These are the guidelines that we use in our church when we are encouraging our community to actively love other people.

Keep everything you do free.

The love that God first showed us was given for free and we believe that we should love other people from the same foundation.

Most of the practical love ideas we have suggested can be done for no, or little cost, and we have found that doing them for free creates a great starting point for conversation.

Do it with other people.

We believe that God created us to journey in life together as a community. Many of these practical love ideas provide an opportunity to get other people involved - whether they are Christians or not. Most people have an innate desire to help others. Remember the story we told about our friend who came to India to help people less fortunate than himself and through that experience encountered the love of God by being around other Christians.

"And you should imitate me, just as I imitate Christ."

(1 Corinthians 11:1)

We think this is a principle to live day-to-day life by. Finding ways to invite others into the normal routines of your life, allows people a chance to see God's love in action.

Think about how you can involve other members of your family.

We find that this is a great way to model Christian living to your children.

It's amazing to see how when you have all generations involved in these acts of love, each generation can reach out to different parts of the community in different ways. It really helps to break down barriers when you have younger and older people involved.

Think about safety and responsibility.

Don't undertake any act of love idea that you don't have the right skills or tools to complete.

If you are outside make sure you wear a hat and sunscreen and always drink enough water.

If you have children or teenagers involved, make sure their parents are there, or have given consent and that suitably qualified supervisors are available.

If appropriate, make sure you have got any relevant permissions from local businesses and government agencies.

Stay humble.

It's easy to have an "us" and "them" attitude with the people you are reaching out to. You can feel that you're special because you are doing something generous to help someone else. Jesus has something to say about that kind of thinking:

> *"Watch out! Don't do your good deeds publicly, to be admired by others, for you will lose the reward from your Father in heaven. When you give to someone in need, don't do as the hypocrites do - blowing trumpets in the synagogues and streets to call attention to their acts of charity! I tell you the truth, they have received all the reward they will ever get. But when you give to someone in need, don't let your left hand know what your right hand is doing. Give your gifts in private, and your Father, who sees everything, will reward you." (Matthew 6:1-4)*

Make sure it is clear that there are no obligations.

People will often be suspicious in the first instance. You might hear words like "What's the catch?" You need to have a genuine desire to love people, as any false motives will be seen through very quickly.

Don't push the name of your church or organisation.

We are not trying to get people to come to our church, we are trying to get them to realise there is a God who loves them. If you make this about church promotion, people will question what other agendas you have.

We only give people the name of our church if they ask about it and if they do, we usually have some information we can give them.

Never give people money directly.

If people are asking for money, there is usually a reason they need it, in which case we will try and help with that need rather than giving them money. Often the option of providing a meal, buying some basic groceries or fuel can help in these situations.

Be prepared to give an answer

Inevitably you will get asked "Why are you doing this?" or "Is it really free - what's the catch?" Building relationships through practical love is a big part of what this is all about. Peter wrote in one of his letters:

> *"And if someone asks about your Christian hope, always be ready to explain it. But do this in a gentle and respectful way." (1 Peter 3:15-16)*

Don't waste the opportunity to engage in conversation - make sure you know what you will say when this happens.

We would often say that we are trying to show God's love in a practical way and we don't just want to be a church that talks about this without any practical action. You'll be surprised where the conversation goes!

Categories

We have defined a number of categories that are scripturally based on the different areas God calls us to love other people.

The description below gives details and scriptures for each category and why we think it is relevant to loving people.

Community

Many of these ideas help you and your church or organisation have a positive impact in your community. We believe that the church should be a pillar in society – to the point that if you weren't there, your community would notice a big difference.

> "You are the light of the world - like a city on a hilltop that cannot be hidden. No one lights a lamp and then puts it under a basket. Instead, a lamp is placed on a stand, where it gives light to everyone in the house. In the same way let your good deeds shine out for all to see, so that everyone will praise your heavenly Father." (Matthew 5:14-16)

We are to be the light of the world and Jesus says one of the ways we are to do this is by our good deeds - in a way that all can see.

The Community category includes any idea that will help you have a positive impact in your community.

Creation

If we want to love other people, we need to look after the world in which we all live. God has given us responsibility to look after the earth and by doing this we are loving people now and in generations to come. The earth is part of what God has created - so why wouldn't we want to look after it?

> *"When I look at the night sky and see the work of your fingers, the moon and the stars you set in place, what are mere mortals that you should think about them, human beings that you should care for them? Yet you made them only a little lower than God and crowned them with glory and honour. You gave them charge of everything you made, putting all things under their authority - the flocks and the herds and all the wild animals, the birds in the sky, the fish in the sea, and everything that swims the ocean currents."*
> *(Psalm 8:3-8)*

Creation also points people towards God. While we want to worship the Creator and not creation, we need to realise that people can find God through the things He has made.

> *"For ever since the world was created, people have seen the earth and sky. Through everything God made, they can clearly see his invisible qualities - his eternal power and divine nature. So they have no excuse for not knowing God."* (Romans 1:20)

The Creation category includes any ideas that are about looking after the earth and living in a sustainable way that minimises our impact on the environment.

Elderly

The elderly are those in our community who have paved the way before us. In their older years they are often battling with health issues and sometimes with loneliness, as many of their friends and family begin to pass away. We need to be finding ways to show practical love to them and to help them make sure they are right with God in their last days.

> *"Never speak harshly to an older man, but appeal to him respectfully as you would to your own father. Talk to younger men as you would to your own brothers. Treat older women as you would your mother, and treat younger women with all purity as you would your own sisters. Take*

care of any widow who has no one else to care for her."

(1 Timothy 5:1-3)

The Elderly category includes any ideas that are about loving the elderly in your community.

Encouragement

Spontaneous generosity in word or action can bring unexpected joy into someone's day. People often find that their day is full of things that discourage them, so a great way to love other people is to take the time to encourage them.

> *"Let everything you say be good and helpful, so that your words will be an encouragement to those who hear them."*
> *(Ephesians 4:29)*

The Encouragement category includes any idea that allows you to speak or write words of encouragement to people in your community.

Family

If we want to love other people, then it needs to start in our own home. We are passionate about seeing healthy, functioning families and we need to be loving other people in a way that supports family relationships.

We also encourage getting all generations involved in loving other people. This is a great way to model Christian living to your children. In addition, when you are reaching out to other people as a family unit, each generation can reach out to different parts of the community in their own way.

> *"But those who won't care for their relatives, especially those in their own household, have denied the true faith. Such people are worse than unbelievers." (1 Timothy 5:8)*

The Family category includes any idea that involves all members of the family or supports the development of a healthy, functioning family.

Health

When someone suffers any form of sickness, there is a clear opportunity to reach out and love them in practical ways.

We need to remember that Jesus calls us to pray for the sick.

> *"One day Jesus called together his twelve disciples and gave them power and authority to cast out all demons and to heal all diseases. Then he sent them out to tell everyone about the Kingdom of God and to heal the sick." (Luke 9:1-2)*

It also becomes difficult for you to love other people when you are not in good health yourself. Make sure that as you reach out to meet the needs of other people you are also looking after your own health.

> *"Don't you realise that your body is the temple of the Holy Spirit, who lives in you and was given to you by God? You do not belong to yourself, for God bought you with a high price. So you must honour God with your body."*
>
> *(1 Corinthians 6:19-20)*

The Health category includes any idea that helps to improve someone's physical or emotional health.

Homeless

The homeless are often marginalised in our society. Our experience has been that we shouldn't assume the needs of the homeless as simply being what appears an obvious need of shelter. A more common need we have found with this group is the desire for conversation and being part of community, having a place where they belong.

> *"Free those who are wrongly imprisoned, lighten the burden of those who work for you. Let the oppressed go free, and remove the chains that bind people. Share your food with the hungry, and give shelter to the homeless. Give clothes to*

those who need them, and do not hide from relatives who need your help." (Isaiah 58:6-7)

The Homeless category includes any idea that provides a way to love the homeless.

Poor

Clearly God cares about the poor and it's often this group that comes to mind when people think about loving others. While we should direct a lot of attention to the physically poor because there are so many scriptures that call us to do this - we should also consider those who seem to have all they need in a material sense but are spiritually poor.

"Their trust should be in God, who richly gives us all we need for our enjoyment. Tell them to use their money to do good. They should be rich in good works and generous to those in need, always being ready to share with others. By doing this they will be storing up their treasure as a good foundation for the future so that they may experience true life." (1 Timothy 6:17-19)

The Poor category includes any idea that is about helping those less fortunate than you, both in your own community as well as those who are the poorest of the poor in third-world nations.

Spiritual

We can love people through our own spiritual disciplines. This might be by praying for people or by helping them on their own spiritual journey.   There are a growing number of people who have an agnostic view towards spirituality, so this can simply be about finding ways to get them to explore the meaning of life and pointing them towards God.

> *"Train yourself to be godly. Physical training is good, but training for godliness is much better, promising benefits in this life and in the life to come." (1 Timothy 4:7-9)*

This category is also about us motivating one another, in a spiritual sense, to love other people.

> *"Let us think of ways to motivate one another to acts of love and good works." (Hebrews 10:24)*

The Spiritual category includes any idea that is about praying for people or living spiritual disciplines that will help point people towards God.

Technology

We live in a world where more and more people are interacting online. Social media creates an environment where people with common interests can find a way to connect and communicate with each other.   It's about relationships.   We believe it represents a place where we should be loving people. A place to engage with, keep up with and influence with the love of God.

> *"Yes, I try to find common ground with everyone, doing everything I can to save some. I do everything to spread the Good News and share in its blessings."*
>
> *(1 Corinthians 9:22-23)*

The Technology category includes any idea that is either about using technology to love other people or giving up technology to gain an appreciation of what others go without, to help in how we reach out to them.

Workplace

When looking at ways to love other people we look at groups like the poor, the homeless or the sick. However, for many of us, God has placed us in the marketplace (government, education or business) and we need to find ways to love people in our workplace.

> *"Work willingly at whatever you do, as though you were working for the Lord rather than for people. Remember that*

the Lord will give you an inheritance as your reward, and that the Master you are serving is Christ."

(Colossians 3:23-24)

The Workplace category includes any idea that relates to reaching out and loving people in your workplace.

Individual or Group

For each idea we have listed, it has been marked to show whether it is something that you can do on your own and/or with other people, using the following symbols:

 Individual

 Group

A great test of integrity is to ask yourself "who am I when no one is watching me?" It can be easy to ignore opportunities to love other people when you're on your own, so we have presented many ideas that you can use in your own daily life.

However, we also believe that God didn't intend us to do the journey of life on our own. Rather, we are meant to do it with others - as community. We have also presented a whole range of group ideas as we have found that there is so much more momentum (and fun) when you get groups together and find creative ways to love other people.

Practical love ideas

Community

Pick up the rubbish in your neighbourhood street.

Set up a free carwash with some friends for a day.

Have a day of cooking with friends to freeze meals for people who need them.

Be kind to someone who isn't kind to you.

Volunteer your skills to a communtiy group for a day.

Tell the cleaner at the local shopping centre what a great job they do.

Adopt a local park with friends and help keep it clean.

Drop off morning tea to the local police station.

Buy groceries from a local business rather than the big chain.

Run or walk in a charity race with friends.

Offer free gift-wrapping at a local shopping centre.

Give drinks away at a traffic stoplight.

Carpool with other people to work or school.

Invite a new neighbour to your home for dinner.

Pray for your local government leaders.

Smile and greet everyone you see today.

Wash the windows of a local business.

Volunteer at the local animal shelter.

Give a lift to someone who needs transport.

Start a regular running or walking group.

Buy someone tickets to a local music or sporting event.

Make someone laugh.

Bring in your neighbour's rubbish bin for them.

Pray for your local school teachers.

Tip a fast food worker.

Gather old mobile phones and donate them to a men's or women's shelter.

Send a thankyou card to a local mission organisation.

Take hot chocolate to those waiting for the bus.

Offer to do some gardening for a neighbour. 👤

Send an email encouraging your local member of parliament. 👤

Search the internet to educate yourself about the poor in your community. 👤

At Christmas time sing carols at a nursing home. 👥

Buy hardware supplies from your local hardware store rather than the big chain. 👤

Send an encouraging card to a local school teacher. 👤

Wash your neighbour's car. 👤

Walk and pray around your neighbourhood. 👤 👥

Drop in morning tea to the local fire station. 👥

Buy stamps and give them away in front of the post office you bought them from.

Read a book to a young child, a blind person or an older neighbour.

Clean up graffiti in your community.

Collect children's books for the needy.

Arrange to have a meal with a few households in your neighbourhood.

Nominate and vote for someone in your local communtiy citizen awards.

Pray for your local businesses.

Buy your fruit and vegetables from the local farmers market.

Write a thankyou note to an old teacher or lecturer. 👤

Collect old clothes and donate them for a dress-up area at a local daycare centre. 👤 👥

Volunteer to clean up rubbish at a commnity event. 👤 👥

Send an encouraging note to a local business leader. 👤

Buy music from a local artist. 👤

Drop into your neighbour's house for a chat. 👤

Volunteer at a local after-school program. 👤

Help clean up a neighbour's garden. 👤 👥

Help fix a run down playground. 👥

Make a new friend.

Buy a small gift for the checkout operator at your local grocery store.

Volunteer to help at a charity auction.

Set up a prayer table at a local community event.

Offer to clean windscreens for free at the local petrol station.

Host an international student.

Buy and give away a copy of the local newspaper.

Ask someone about their family history.

Send someone flowers to brighten their day.

Remember to say thank you. 👤

Collect magazines and donate them to daycare centres or local doctors surgeries. 👤👥

Encourage the local school canteen to donate leftover food to local shelters. 👤

Be courteous as you drive on the roads. 👤

Join your local neighbourhood watch program. 👤

Volunteer at an agency that works with children with disabilities. 👤👥

Take photos during a communtiy event and donate them to the event organisers. 👤👥

Offer your skills to someone for free. 👤

Assist at an after-school sports program. 👤

Donate and decorate a Christmas tree for a nursing home, hospital or homeless shelter.

Offer a free sausage sizzle at a local community event.

Offer to escort shoppers to their cars with an umbrella on a rainy day.

Stop a gossiping conversation.

Offer lollies to retail workers on busy days.

Give drinks away at a local sports event.

Rake up leaves on gardens in your community.

Offer to pack groceries at your local grocery store.

Renew an old friendship.

Clean a neighbour's or eldery person's home.

Ask someone who comes from another country about their culture.

Set up a drinks station on a local walking trail.

Ask neighbours if they would like to be on a street phone and email list, to share with each other for safety.

Creation

Buy your fruit and vegetables from the local farmers market.

Go bag free for your grocery shopping.

Carpool with other people to school or work.

Take time to watch the sunrise or the sunset.

Have a shorter shower.

Grow something you can eat.

Use less paper.

Dress for the season before using heating and cooling systems.

Use chemical free cleaning products.

Turn lights off when you are not using them.

Ride your bike to school or work.

Use your own drink bottle rather than buying bottled water.

Use biodegradable plastic bags in your bins.

Go on a hike and admire creation.

Choose to buy organic or free-range eggs.

Volunteer at an animal shelter.

Use more energy efficient lights.

Plant a tree.

Gaze at the stars at night and read Psalm 8.

Remember to use your environmental grocery shopping bags.

Don't use the stand-by power for TV's and computers.

Use the half-flush on the toilet.

Choose to buy organic or free-range meat.

Use the recycling collection service from your local government.

Measure your carbon footprint and find a way to offset your carbon emissions.

Set up your own composting bin for food scraps.

Take the stairs instead of the lift.

Use recycled materials where available.

Elderly

Visit the elderly in an aged care facility and take the time to have a conversation with them. 👤👥

Make birthday cards for the elderly you know. 👤👥

Give a lift to someone who needs transport. 👤

At Christmas time sing carols at a nursing home. 👥

Teach a senior friend how to use a computer. 👤

Do something to recognise war veterans in your community. 👥

Put on afternoon tea at a nursing home. 👥

Clean a neighbour's or elderly person's house. 👤👥

Ask someone about their family history. 👤

Encouragement

Write an encouraging note to your parents.

Pay for a stranger's coffee or tea next time you are in a coffee shop.

Make get well cards for people in hospitals.

Send someone an encouraging e-card.

Renew an old friendship.

Let someone go in front of you in a long line.

Buy groceries from the local business rather than the big chain.

Drop off morning tea to the local police station.

Write a thankyou letter to an old teacher or lecturer.

Use no negative words for a day.

Pay for the meal of the person behind you at a fast-food drive-thru.

Send an encouraging note to a local business leader.

Make birthday cards for the elderly.

Tell the cleaner at your local shopping centre what a great job they do.

Send someone flowers to brighten their day.

Make it common practice for you to give people the benefit of the doubt.

Take someone who is lonely to the movies.

Send a card to someone who needs encouragement.

Nominate and vote for someone in your local community citizen awards.

Buy a tank of fuel for a student you know.

Have lunch with a co-worker who you don't know very well.

Make a positive comment on a website or blog.

Tip your waiter or waitress generously.

Send a thankyou card to a local mission organisation.

Send an email encouraging your local member for parliament.

Give money to a street performer.

Stop a gossiping conversation.

Pay for a stranger's fuel, as well as yours, when you next fill up your car.

Send a card encouraging your local school teacher.

Buy hardware supplies from the local business rather than the big chain.

Family

Sponsor a child from a third world nation.

Collect old clothes and donate them for a dress-up area at a daycare centre.

Babysit for free so some parents you know can have a date night.

Write an encouraging note to your parents.

Buy a gift for a single mother on mother's day.

Read a book to a young child, a blind person or an older neighbour.

Organise a "get to know you" lunch for new neighbours in your neighbourhood.

Make gifts with friends for children in hospital.

Work with disabled children on an art project.

Honour your parents.

Ask someone about their family history.

Collect old sports equipment and donate it to needy families.

Volunteer at an agency that works with children with disabilities.

Buy a gift for a single father on father's day.

Donate and decorate a Christmas tree at a nursing home, hospital or homeless shelter.

Collect and donate toys to children in the cancer ward of a hospital.

Volunteer at a local school's "after school" program.

Ask neighbours if they would like to be on a street phone and email list, to share with each other for safety.

Host an international student.

Collect children's books for the needy.

Health

Make a meal for a sick friend.

Drop off groceries for someone who can't get out.

Secretly pay a sick person's medical bill.

Sponsor a child from a third world nation.

Run or walk in a charity race with friends.

Volunteer at an agency that works with children with disabilities.

Clean up a neighbour's garden who cannot do it themselves.

Collect old sports equipment and donate it to needy families.

Ride your bike to school or work.

Break a bad habit.

Set up your own composting bin for scraps.

Choose to buy organic or free range meat.

Pack a bag of medical supplies and give them to a homeless person.

Buy your fruit and vegetables from the local gardeners market.

Have a day of cooking with friends to freeze meals for people who need them.

Donate blood.

Start a regular running or walking group.

Work with disabled children on an art project. 👤👥

Collect and donate toys to children in the cancer ward of a hospital. 👤👥

Clean the house for an injured or sick friend. 👤

Donate old eyeglasses to an organisation that recycles them for the needy. 👤👥

Give a lift to someone who needs transport. 👤

Volunteer at the local hospital. 👤👥

Choose to buy organic or free range eggs. 👤

Pray for someone who is sick. 👤👥

Spend a day without using technology. 👤👥

Grow something you can eat.

Begin to exercise regularly.

Make get-well cards for people in hospital.

Measure your carbon footprint and find a way to offset your carbon emissions.

Visit a rehabilitation centre and volunteer to help patients with special needs.

Make gifts with friends for children in hospital.

Go on a hike and admire creation.

Assist an after-school sports program for children.

Take the stairs instead of the lift.

Homeless

Bake some biscuits and deliver them to a soup kitchen or shelter. 👤👥

Have a coffee or tea with a homeless person. 👤

Encourage the school canteen to donate leftover food to local shelters. 👤

Pack a bag of medical supplies and given them to a homeless person. 👤👥

Use candles instead of lights for a night to experience how some people live. 👤👥

Donate and decorate a Christmas tree at a nursing home, hospital or homeless shelter. 👤👥

Set up a reading hour at a homeless shelter and bring books to share. 👤👥

Pack a bag of toiletries and give to a homeless person.

Donate blankets to a homeless shelter.

Give a phonecard to someone who needs it.

Donate toys and clothes to a shelter.

Have a conversation with a homeless person.

Make a care package with socks, t-shirts and shorts for a child at a shelter.

Drop off some books to a homeless person to read.

Poor

Sponsor a child from a third world country.

Drop off unused clothes to a local clothes collection bin.

Spend one day trying to live off $2.

Sell possessions you don't need and give the funds raised to a charity.

Make a care package with socks, t-shirts and shorts for a child at a shelter.

Keep the TV off for one week to experience life without technology.

Offer your skills to someone for free.

Give a phonecard to someone who needs it.

Donate your spare change to a charitable cause.

Collect old sports equipment and donate it to needy families.

Donate old eyeglasses to an organisation that recycles them for the needy.

Encourage the school canteen to donate leftover food to local shelters.

Collect unused make-up and perfume for a centre for abused women.

Celebrate your birthday by asking for items to donate to a cause, instead of gifts for yourself.

Give a fuel gift card to someone in need.

Drop off a day's groceries to the local foodbank.

Secretly pay a neighbour's electricity bill.

Donate to an organisation that provides water to poor communities.

Gather old mobile phones and donate to a men's or women's shelter.

Use candles instead of lights for a night to experience how some people live.

Buy nothing for a day and give away what you would have spent.

Collect money for a good cause.

Bake some biscuits and deliver to a homeless shelter.

Collect children's books for the needy.

Give a grocery gift card to someone in need.

Donate to an organisation providing micro-finance loans.

Search the internet to educate yourself about the poor in your community.

Donate toys and clothes to a shelter.

Volunteer at a local foodbank.

Donate one day's salary to a charity.

Fast one meal and donate what you would have spent to a local foodbank.

Spiritual

Take a prayer walk around your neighbourhood.

Forgive someone who has hurt or offended you.

Read the book of Acts.

Pray for your local businesses.

Share a verse from the book of Proverbs on Facebook or Twitter.

Meet with some friends and talk through Romans 12.

Pray for someone who is sick.

Pray for opportunity to share the gospel with a friend.

Gaze at the stars at night and read Psalm 8.

Set up a prayer table at a local fair or market.

Pray for your local government leaders.

Read the gospel of Mark in one sitting.

Give your testimony to a friend.

Honour your parents.

Pray for your local school teachers.

Post a thought provoking quote about God on your Facebook or Twitter account.

Meet with some friends and talk through Isaiah 58.

Technology

Send someone an encouraging e-card. 👤

Share a verse from the book of Proverbs on Facebook or Twitter. 👤

Teach a senior friend how to use a computer. 👤

Use less paper. 👤

Make a positive comment on a website or blog. 👤

Search the internet to educate yourself about the poor in your community. 👤

Post a thought provoking quote about God on your Facebook account. 👤

Spend a day without using technology. 👤👤

Workplace

Spontaneously buy morning tea for your co-workers.

Organise a charity day at work.

Stop a gossiping conversation.

Collect your work colleagues lunch dishes - wash and return them.

Carpool with other people to work or school.

Have lunch with a co-worker you don't know very well.

Find some people you can pray with during your lunch break.

Ask someone who comes from another country about their culture.

Be kind to someone who isn't kind to you.

Get people in your workplace to volunteer their expertise to a communtiy agency for a day.

Start a regular running or walking group.

Pray for your boss and your work colleagues.

Invite some work colleagues around for a meal.

Pray for someone who is sick.

The top 5: best group ideas

If you want to get started with some friends we have listed below our Top 5 group ideas. These are cost effective, simple to organise and allow a group to work together in loving other people.

1. Pick up the street litter in your neighbourhood.

2. Set up a free car-wash with some friends.

3. Have a day of cooking with friends to freeze meals ready for when people may need them.

4. Offer to wash the windows for free for local businesses.

5. Set up a free drinks station on a local walking trail.

The top 5: things you can do on your own

If you are looking for simple ways to get started on your own then here are our Top 5 individual ideas. They are simple, either free or very low cost and will give you the chance to start loving someone straight away.

1. Have a conversation with a homeless person.

2. Organise a "get-to-know-you" lunch for people in your neighbourhood.

3. Send a card to someone who needs encouragement.

4. Offer to do some gardening for a neighbour.

5. Make a meal for a sick friend.

Study guide

We have provided a study guide on each chapter from Part A: Love Love below.

The idea is that in a small group you read through the relevant scriptures, discuss the concepts in more detail, and look at how you can apply them in the context of your own life and church or Christian organisation.

Chapter One: Why love love?

Read

Mark 12:30-31

Romans 12:9

Discuss

1. What does it mean to love God with all of your:

   (a) heart

   (b) soul

   (c) mind

   (d) strength?

2. Why do you think God calls us to love other people?

3. Why would Paul say don't pretend to love people?

Notes

Chapter Two: It really works

Read

John 3:16

Romans 12:10-21

Discuss

1. If you are a Christian - how did that happen?

    (a) were friends or family involved

    (b) looking back, what conversations did people have with you that helped

    (c) were there any practical things that people did that helped?

2. In your life right now are there any things you are doing to practically love other people?

Notes

Chapter Three: What started in Vanuatu...

Read

Luke 9:23-27

James 2:14-18

Ephesians 2:8-10

Discuss

1. What does Jesus mean when he says you need to give up your life to save it?

2. Think of examples where you have seen materialism, consumerism, rationalism and hedonism. Why do you think these are issues we need to contend with?

3. What do you think the difference is between going to church and being the church?

4. Do you think we have to work to earn our salvation?

Notes

Chapter Four: God first loved you

Read

1 John 3:16-18

1 John 4:19

Discuss

1. Describe what you think love is?

2. How do you think God has loved us?

3. At the moment what do you do to respond to God's love?

Notes

Chapter Five: Now love one another

Read

1 John 13:34-35

Galatians 6:10

Acts 2:44-45

2 Corinthians 9:11-12

Discuss

1. Why do you think it is important for us to love other Christians?

2. Have you ever had times where other Christians have done something practical to show you love?

3. Have you ever done anything practical to help out another Christian?

Notes

Chapter Six: Why love other people?

Read

Isaiah 58:6-7

1 Corinthians 13:1-3

Matthew 25:44-45

2 Timothy 4:5

2 Corinthians 5:20

Discuss

1. Can you think of practical ways you can love other people:

    (a) on your own

    (b) with other people?

2. Have you ever had the chance to lead someone to the Lord? If you have, describe how that happened. If you haven't think about why not and how you could change that.

Notes

Chapter Seven: What happens when it doesn't work?

Read

Matthew 18:12-14

Luke 6:27-36

Romans 12:17-21

Discuss

1. Describe a time where you have felt your generosity was taken advantage of?

2. What does it feel like to consider loving people who you don't like - maybe someone who has hurt or offended you?

3. How did Jesus respond to loving His enemies?

Notes

Chapter Eight: Local or international?

Read

Matthew 28:18-19

Acts 1:8

Discuss

1. What area would you describe as your Jerusalem (your neighbourhood)?

2. What do you know about the demographics, the local businesses, the schools and the government agencies in your neighbourhood?   How well are you interacting with them?

3. Are there any nations that you have a heart for?

Notes

Chapter Nine: Servant evangelism or power evangelism?

Read

Luke 9:1-2

Acts 3:1-11

Discuss

1. How does the Holy Spirit help us as we are trying to love other people?

2. How is healing and the use of other spiritual gifts an expression of love?

3. How do servant evangelism and power evangelism work together in how we should reach out to other people?

Notes

Chapter Ten: Love. It's simple really.

Read

1 Corinthians 11:1

Hebrews 10:24

Discuss

1. Do you have a heart to love people in your community?

2. What are the first things you can do to start loving other people?

3. Who else can you get involved?

Notes

About the authors

Derek and Kylie Gerrard have been married for 15 years. Together they are the senior ministers at a church in Scarborough, Western Australia called Be The Church (www.bethechurch.org.au), part of the C3 Church movement.

Derek has a Bachelor of Business and is about to complete a Master of Arts in Christian Studies. He has worked in the marketplace as a management consultant for 13 years and currently runs a technology company called Greensense (www.greensense.com.au). He has a passion for social justice and loves to surf and play golf.

Kylie has worked in the Insurance and Finance industries for over 10 years. She loves travelling and experiencing other cultures and has led many teams to third world nations to serve the poor and marginalised. Kylie is passionate about healthy living and fitness and equipping others in this area.

Christian Stuff

If you enjoyed Love Love - then we would like to recommend "Christian Stuff" - another free eBook authored by Derek Gerrard and BTC Publishing. It includes a range of 3 minute videos, scripture and discussion points to help you or a small group get started on exploring what this Christian Stuff is all about.

The topics include:
1. The Bible
2. Creation
3. Separation
4. Jesus
5. The Holy Spirit
6. Church

To get your free copy go to:
www.bethechurch.org.au/christian-stuff

Notes

Notes

CPSIA information can be obtained at www.ICGtesting.com
Printed in the USA
LVOW042146161112

307553LV00004B/1/P

9 780987 414106